Healthy Drinks

First published by Bonnier Fakta, Stockholm, Sweden

The information in this book is provided only as an information resource, and should not be taken as a substitute for medical advice or treatment.

10 9 8 7 6 5 4 3 2 1

Library of Congress Cataloging-in-Publication Data is available on file.

Cover and design by Kai Ristilla
Photography by Helén Pe
Copyright pictures © Hannah Lemholt S. 16 Mö, Bildbyrå/Petter Arvidsson S. 16 MV
Stylist: Sara N. Bergman
Hair and makeup: Josefin Madsen
Visit www.foodpowerforpeople.com.

Print ISBN: 978-1-5107-2350-4
Ebook ISBN: 978-1-5107-2353-5

Printed in China

60 VITAL RECIPES FOR GREEN SMOOTHIES, JUICE SHOTS, BROTHS, DETOX WATER, KOMBUCHA, AND MORE

Healthy Drinks

ANNA OTTOSON

Translated by Gun Penhoat

Photography by Heléne Pe

Skyhorse Publishing

CONTENTS

INDULGE IN GREAT HEALTH
— with no rules

I live. I love. I laugh. And I eat. I think there's nothing more beautiful than a person who feels good in his or her own body. And I'm not talking about pounds and wrinkles. For me, life and healthy food mean possibilities, pleasure, and heading toward a place of radiant energy and an abundance of joy. It's about treating and giving ourselves the best of the best, and doing the best we can. That's why I love healthy drinks: they're such a simple yet liberating way to drink yourself to health. Prep time takes only a few minutes, yet they make a huge difference to your well-being, to how you feel, and to your energy level (you'll shine like a thousand suns!). Also, they taste crazy good.

Super smoothies provide you with amazing daily energy. Juice shots are your best friends come flu season. Refreshing lemonades, juices, and slushies—they're all totally sugar-free. Warm broths feel like great big hugs, especially when you need them the most. Or a wonderfully healthy hot chocolate, made with real chocolate, can make you believe you're gazing deep into Johnny Depp's eyes in the movie *Chocolat*.

I grew up in a family of hard-core exercisers. Running thirty to thirty-five miles a week and putting in a three-hour road session on Sundays was part of my life. It just wasn't worth lacing up your sneakers for anything less than six miles. From these beginnings blossomed a keen interest in how what we eat can affect athletic performance. As a young girl, I stayed in my room slurping up every book on nutrition I could find, long before the current health craze hit. At sixteen, I realized this was my destiny, which defined my academic path during my four years at university and ultimately my career. This would be my Dharma—my life's purpose.

But that's not the whole truth. There's another story, one about confronting death head on and the fear of loss. The school of hard knocks has shaped me to the core

and defined what I believe in. As a kid, I would visit my mother after her radiation treatment and be utterly convinced that she would not survive to see my eighteenth birthday. I have had close encounters with cancer all my life. Friends have become angels. Life is a roller-coaster ride, filled with exhilarating experiences, along with a few seriously nasty bumps. These two parallel journeys have led up to this point in my life and what I'm all about today: working in the world of food and health. It's also one of the reasons why I founded Foodpowers, a rehabilitation program for cancer survivors.

It's important for me to seize the day. I like to let my hair down and let myself go, to dance on the table like there's no tomorrow. I am fully and totally dedicated to working with food, health, and all the amazing ways there are to live healthily.

For me, these healthy drinks have been totally groundbreaking; in our home, drinking them is second nature. It's an easy way for the kids to get the nutrients they need, even if they pick at their dinner.

Stop dieting. Quit the rules. There is *nothing* you *must do*. We're pressured into counting calories till we're blue in the face, or we're dieting our precious lives away. I believe that life is too short to be on a diet. It's a bit like walking around in too-tight shoes: they're just never going to fit *you* and your life. So instead of zeroing in on what you *can't* eat, focus on all the other options that are out there, the many tasty possibilities you can enjoy that will bless you with a radiant, vibrant energy to live the life you long for. Drink yourself healthy. Add one healthy drink to your day—it'll take you *so* far. The quickest recipe in this book can be prepared in a minute—just like brushing your teeth. *Let's blend together!*

Green love from
Anna Ottosson, a.k.a. Madame Moustache

FOOD SUPERPOWERS

What *Foodpower* means to me is eating and enjoying food that makes us radiant and stronger.

The food we eat holds enormous power. The tears rolling down our cheeks as we chop onions, our pee turning pink after eating beets, our tongue colors stained blue by blueberries—those are all visible signs of how much we're affected by the foods we enjoy. Nutrition research from all over the world shows that we can boost our immune system and protect ourselves from illness in an incredibly potent way via our food. We know that over 30 percent of all cancers are connected to our eating habits. Thousands of antioxidants protect and build up our body, and neutralize free radicals to prevent them from damaging our cells. But you don't need to study all of this—just enjoy fruit and vegetables in all the colors of the rainbow, and get into the habit of knocking back a colorful healthy drink every day. By doing this, you will have already taken a large dose of beneficial power that will build up your defenses against colds, heightened stress, and the rest of life.

The rainbow is truly an amazing guide to follow when selecting your food—it's the only one I use. **Make your food colorful, and you'll leave behind all shades of brown!** By eating a variety of vibrantly colorful foods, you'll receive lots of vitamins, antioxidants, minerals, and other powerful nutrients effortlessly.

Enjoy—tickle your taste buds and totally love yourself, because there is only one precious *you*. Eat and drink food that gives you real, deep, and long-lasting energy. Inside-out. For real.

"You are what you eat. Don't be fast, cheap, easy, or fake."

HEALTHY DRINKS—A SIMPLE WAY TO MAXIMIZE YOUR HEALTH

Do you want to make a single change that will have maximum impact on your health? That's as quick and easy as A-B-C? Then this is for you. I get asked this question every day, and my answer is: start with healthy drinks. They provide a huge health boost and are a simple habit to work into your daily routine. BAM! Let's go . . . set the blender in the middle of your kitchen like a lighthouse, so it will be a lovely reminder every time you walk by it.

The gateway to healthy drinks is typically through fruity, sweeter smoothies, but afterward we often move on to greener, more hard-core varieties, that luckily have rather addictive qualities! You can turn up and down their sweetness to suit your taste by adding more or fewer natural sweet ingredients. Continue experimenting with green smoothies, one per day (a day without a green smoothie is a lost day), and notice the amazing difference in yourself—many say they feel more radiant and energized, and they have less cravings for sweets. Don't forget to check out your skin, too. Later, expand your repertoire by throwing back juice shots, sipping detox water, enjoying comforting broths, and drinking refreshing healthy lemonades.

I use organic produce whenever I can and choose nature's own plant-based ingredients over powders and extracts. My ingredients never contain added sugar—no white sugar, agave syrup, or artificial sweeteners.

Buy your favorite foods at the farmers' market or your local grocery store, or start your new life with the click of a mouse and get a box of organic produce shipped right to your doorstep. The effect healthy drinks will have on your life will amaze you.

RECIPES—LIBERATING AND EASYGOING

This book covers everything—from made-in-a-flash recipes to broths that simmer for days. This is the most liberating and easygoing food prep you can imagine. Not much can go wrong here. Just go for it! Whether you're using the blender or a stockpot, this type of food is extremely effortless, and you'll transform into a star in the kitchen.

Most of these smoothie recipes make four servings, while the juice shots typically serve two. The reason is simply that I've chosen to make larger quantities of drinks that can be put into your favorite to-go glass bottle, jar, or mug, while it's best to down the smaller quantities of drinks on the spot. When you make broth, make sure to cook lots of it, though, as it's not worth simmering stock for days to only make a few cups. In this case, the more the merrier.

The recipes make up a bunch of irresistible healthy drinks, each with their own specific health benefits, and every one of them is a favorite of mine! Go ahead, try them, and discover your own personal fave. Don't be afraid—spread your wings and be inspired to try out your own healthy drinks. Go easy on the strong flavors, however: too much of a good thing can be wonderful, but it can also cross the line from delicious to inedible. Always start by adding the smallest quantity of an ingredient with an intense taste when you make a healthy drink for the first time; that way, you'll know at what point you can add more zing.

"I kiss better than I cook"

THE PANTRY & ITS TOOLS

MY SUPERSTARS

Keeping a bunch of superstars on hand at home makes your kitchen feel like a walk-in closet because you don't need to go shopping for groceries every time a craving hits or when you're in a hurry. You'll benefit every day from using this list, either as a shopping guide or as a cheat sheet for different *foodpowers*.

Baby spinach: packed with iron and nitrates; a runners' darling
Ginger: anti-inflammatory, antioxidant; will scare off colds
Turmeric: contains the colorant curcumin, which is anti-inflammatory, anti-carcinogenic, and a strong antioxidant
Avocado: great source of fatty acids, provides a delectable sense of satiety
Beets: loaded with nitrates
Ruby red grapefruit: rich in vitamin C; a powerful citrus fruit that also contains the super antioxidant lycopene as a secret ingredient
Chaga: super mushrooms, with extremely high levels of antioxidants
Blueberries: vitamin blockbusters, anti-inflammatory
Acai: the Amazon's blueberry
Almonds: rich in vitamin E and magnesium

I prefer to eat real, natural food instead of using powders. However, there's a whole world of natural super ingredients in powder form that you can try if you'd like to add more power to your smoothies. Here are a few of them, and where they fit best:
With green drinks: chlorella, spirulina
With chocolate: maca root
With colorful ingredients: rose-hip powder, bee pollen

Power blender/mixer

This is necessary for making smoothies and also if you want to whip up a soup or just chop ingredients finely. Go for the most expensive model you can afford. Cheap blenders tend to break down faster; however, a cheap blender is better than no blender at all. If you have one in the cupboard and it isn't top of the line, it'll still do. Prep time will take a bit longer because you'll need to chop the ingredients more finely and add the denser ingredients first. Always start at the highest speed to make sure the ingredients blend properly. To get really smooth almond milk, you'll need a blender with a powerful motor.

Juice extractor and centrifugal juicer

There are two types of juicers: those that crush and those that centrifuge. There are lots of manufacturers, sizes, and price levels; choose one that suits your goals and budget.

Juice extractors crush and grind vegetables and fruit, then press them through a fine-mesh sieve, so choose a model that is easy to use and to clean and that preferably presses at a low speed, such as a cold press juicer or slow juicer—juice extracted more slowly is believed to inhibit oxidation. A juice extractor produces more juice but works more slowly and can't handle large amounts of ingredients at a time, unlike a centrifugal juicer.

Centrifugal juicers grate vegetables and fruits on a large grating surface that spins at a high speed. The juice is extracted by the centrifugal force through a fine net.

Whichever machine is better for you is purely a matter of personal preference.

TIP! Choose a blender that comes with a tamper tool, which makes it easier to blend frozen bananas.

Healthy drinks from morning 'till night!

MORNING: Juice shot and green smoothie for breakfast; store leftovers in a glass bottle for later

DURING THE DAY: Ginger water, vitamin water, or chaga tea instead of tap water; green smoothie instead of coffee and a cookie for your 3 p.m. snack

EVENING: Broth, golden milk

SUGAR CRAVING: Two-layer smoothie

THE DRINKS

Green smoothies

Green smoothies are fantastic because they give you so much vitality and energy. The base is always a vegetable, such as baby spinach. Unlike old-school smoothies, green smoothies don't contain any dairy products as filler—they are completely vegan and are therefore naturally lactose-free. If you're not used to it, drinking green smoothies can seem a bit "hard-core" in the beginning. Your first time might remind you of a "flavor bungee jump." But don't worry—it will soon become a drink you'll long for.

Mixing in an avocado is perfect for making a lovely, creamy green smoothie, and it will provide you with good fats and feelings of satiety. It will also give the smoothie that irresistible and almost sinful creamy quality—like a milk shake. I also like to add in some immunity-boosting ginger, as well as lime and orange juice.

This is the base for almost all green smoothies, which you can also top off with fruit and berries for a sweeter taste, depending on what you feel like and what's in season.

Why not make a larger quantity than you need? Leftovers are perfect for a snack, or if dinner is late hitting the table. They're also easy to put in a to-go bottle. If a recipe calls for limes and oranges, always peel them before adding them to the other ingredients.

Vitamin and detox water

Why settle for tap water or expensive bottled "vitamin water," which also contains a lot of added sugar? Make your own vitamin and detox water that will truly strengthen your body and clean out what the body doesn't need anymore. Before this, you probably perked up your water with lemon wedges or cucumber slices, but why skimp on nutrients when you can go all out and add lots and lots of berries and herbs? Once you've finished the water, eat the berries!

This is a natural vitamin water that keeps away all added refined sugars, sweeteners, or additives, all while it nourishes us with the goodies we love to feed our bodies—pure, wholesome, plant-based ingredients.

Juice shots

These drinks are my darlings—I absolutely love them—but they're not for weaklings. It's simply pure nutrition down your throat. These shots can save you when you feel you are about to be taken down by a nasty cold. It's *foodpower*—literally and figuratively.

There are no long, complicated lists of ingredients; just a few powerful components whose only purpose is to boost you up. A juice shot is a concentrate of antioxidants, trace elements, and vitamins that go straight down the hatch. I love drinking a strong shot first thing in the morning and really *wake up.*

Here, small quantities are the order of the day; don't mix up big batches of juice shots to save for later. The whole point is to drink these ingredients immediately so you don't lose any nutrients.

So why not have another shot? You won't get a hangover!

Health tonics

Drink tonics as an alternative or a complement to juice and smoothies when you feel you need an extra nutrient boost. This isn't what you top your gin with; a health tonic is like an upgrade in today's world of juice and smoothies. It's based on wisdom passed down like a gift through generations of gurus, shamans, and Ayurveda practitioners; from mothers to daughters. Health tonics contain everything from Chinese herbs to Indian superfoods.

During my travels all over the world, I've collected unique riches and life elixirs from different cultures and used them to create the health tonics you see in this book today for your enjoyment.

Super smoothies and two-layer super smoothies

Super smoothies, loaded with colorful fruits and berries, are a simple yet excellent example of rainbow-colored food. Just like a green smoothie, super smoothies are totally dairy-free, with an almond or coconut milk base. They are so incredibly beautiful and delicious that they easily stand in for dessert and ice cream! Whenever I yearn for something sweet, I sometimes replace chocolate pralines with a super smoothie.

If you want to go all-out, make a delicious two-layer smoothie—a smoothie extravaganza as well as a completely healthy decadence.

Juices, healthy lemonades, and slushies

This entire chapter is a feast. Here you'll find juices and wonderfully healthy lemonades, *completely* without added sugar! There are delicious alcohol-free options that are so good they put rosé wine to shame. And, finally, slushies—those refreshing drinks tailor-made for kids' parties or aperitifs for the children at the dinner table—without any artificial colorants and additives. If all your produce is organic, you can juice the fruit without peeling it (this applies to fruits like apples, not oranges, which you still have to peel!).

Madame
MOUSTACHE

Kombucha

Kombucha is a traditional Asian drink made from tea fermented with yeast and bacteria. Its consumption can be traced way back to the emperors of early far-eastern dynasties. These days, especially among health trendsetters, kombucha has overtaken soda as the favorite drink of the rich and famous.

The base for making your own kombucha is a *scoby* (Symbiotic Culture of Bacteria and Yeast), sometimes called "the mother." Ask for it at well-stocked health food stores, or buy it online.

Basically, you must tend to the mother, and if you care for it right it can be reused many times over. The scoby lives and reproduces by making "babies."

Making your own kombucha is much easier than it seems. All you need is tea (black or green), bacteria culture, sugar (no worries, the scoby will eat up the sugar), and patience. You can drink kombucha plain or season it with raspberries, pineapple, cherries, strawberries, or peaches, which are all great flavors to complement the drink. My own favorites are mango, apple, and ginger—you'll find recipes further along in the book.

Chaga

Chaga is the king of medicinal mushrooms. It is rumored to have the highest ORAC-value (the most antioxidants) among other ingredients, far higher in fact than blueberries and cranberries, which also rank at the top. You can buy chaga at well-stocked health food stores or online. You can buy it in small chunks, ground into powder, or as tea. You can drink chaga tea instead of coffee or regular tea, or you can add it to your smoothie for extra flavor and energy.

Chaga is a mushroom that grows wild on birch trees and can be easily spotted on the trees' trunks by its carbonized-looking surface and orangey-brown interior. It is harvested during the fall and winter, up until the trees' sap starts running. Cut the mushroom off the tree, but leave about 20 percent of it behind on the trunk. Only harvest mushrooms from living trees. Don't forget to ask permission from the landowner before harvesting any mushrooms.

Golden milk and other wonderful, warm healthy drinks

While golden milk is super trendy in the West, it is in fact an old Ayurvedic healing drink from India. It's an amazing beverage thanks to its superstar ingredient, turmeric. I often enjoy cupping my hands around a golden milk latte in the evening before bedtime; it goes down gently and smoothly into the stomach as I take a mindful moment to sit and gather the impressions of the day. You'll also find that little gems, such as a matcha tea lattes and wonderful hot chocolates, can awaken the deepest soulful feelings. This chapter offers everything from vital healthy drinks to more grounding and warming chai-moments. Make and drink these whenever you want.

Broth

Broth is like a warm hug. Wrap your hands around a cup or a to-go mug of warm broth on a cold winter's morning, and allow the warming liquid gold to flow down your throat. Broth provides you with wholesome minerals and collagen, which is fantastic for your skin— it can affect and help the skin retain its natural collagen and elasticity, keeping your complexion clear for longer. Bone broth is also good for joints and ligaments.

To be honest, the chapter on broth departs a little from my motto and criteria for healthy living–that it should be quick and easy (preparing a healthy drink should take as long as brushing your teeth!). The process of making broth is definitely not a quick process. However, these broths have earned their place in this book because they are super nutritious and good for you, and they're the perfect warm beverage for the colder season that complements the other smoothies and healthy drinks.

These broths are made entirely from natural ingredients. They are gluten- and dairy-free, and simple to prepare at home. Traditionally, broth is used as the foundation of many different dishes, and salt is never initially included when cooking broth from scratch as you typically need to be able to season the broth afterward. But if you're going to make broth just for drinking, I like to include salt.

You can drink broth plain or with some sea salt, ginger, or chili, or you can use the broth as a base for whatever soup you're craving. A good broth will make you the king or queen in your kitchen. By the way, broth is also great base for sauce.

I simmer broths for a long time to extract all the minerals from the bones and impart flavor and nutrition to the broth. *Don't panic–it's organic.* Cook your broth on a rainy Sunday while sliding around in your knitted socks and hanging out in your pajamas. Let the bone broth simmer on the stove while you crawl back to bed and binge-watch your favorite series.

You'll find bones for sale or available to order at larger grocery stores with a meat counter. If you're lucky enough to have a butcher in your neighborhood, ask for bones, preferably organic. Shin bones and femurs with large quantities of marrow will release a lot of collagen; you can also try bones that are a bit jellied, like oxtail. Ask to have them cut into 4- to 8-inch pieces.

GREEN SMOOTHIES

Everyone, from age one to one hundred, can drink green smoothies. Make green smoothies a daily habit, and you'll notice a huge difference. You are warmly welcomed to a big green smoothie party; let's blend and get ready for a green moustache!

MADAME MOUSTACHE'S GREEN SMOOTHIE

- SERVES 4 -

I like to use dewy, fresh baby spinach leaves that are packed with nitrates, as they will optimally oxygenate the blood. It's like taking a deep yoga breath. Eating more spinach daily will help you run better, whether in the office or on the trail.

2½ oz (70 g) baby spinach (1 bag)
1 avocado
¾–1-inch piece of fresh ginger, peeled
1 banana
1 apple, core removed
⅘ cup (200 ml) orange juice
Juice of 1 lime
Water

Put all the ingredients in a blender. Blend, and add water until it reaches the desired consistency. I love a delicious, thick, creamy texture, but you can add more water if you like.

TIP! Mix the denser ingredients like avocado, ginger, and banana first, then top them with the feather-light baby spinach leaves.

AVOCADO ATTRACTION
- SERVES 4 -

2 avocados
2½ oz (70 g) baby spinach (1 bag)
4½ oz (125 g) frozen mango
¾–2-inch piece of fresh ginger, peeled
Juice of 1 lime
$^2/_5$–$^4/_5$ cup (100–200 ml) orange juice

Blend—and fall in love with this heavenly goddess smoothie.

OOH BABY CHILD
- SERVES 4 -

1 avocado
1 banana
2½ oz (70 g) baby spinach (1 bag)
1 lime
¾–1-inch piece of fresh ginger, peeled
1 handful of frozen peas
1 apple
$^4/_5$ cup (200 ml) orange juice
Water, to desired consistency

Slice the avocado and banana into chunks, put them in the blender with the remaining ingredients, and blend to a creamy consistency. Pour into four glasses and serve right away.

GREEN LOVE
- SERVES 4 -

1 chunk of fennel
1 handful of spinach
1 avocado
¾–1-inch piece of fresh ginger, peeled
1 pear
1 banana
Mint leaves
$^4/_5$ cup (200 ml) orange juice
Water, to desired consistency

Blend it all into a nicely soft smoothie.

GREEN MOUSTACHE

- SERVES 4 -

Often, you'll want to begin with a sweeter taste as you start out drinking smoothies, which is why I've included some mango. However, if you wish to avoid the sweet flavor, add more stalks of broccoli or reduce the amount of mango.

1 stalk of broccoli
1 avocado
1 handful of frozen mango
¾–1-inch piece of fresh ginger, peeled
2½ oz (70 g) baby spinach (1 bag)
Juice of one lime
⁴⁄₅ cup (200 ml) orange juice
Water, to desired consistency

Mix the denser ingredients, like broccoli and avocado, in the blender first, and follow up with the remaining ingredients.

MR. KING

- SERVES 4 -

Kale is the king of the garden. This absolute vegetable superstar contains lots of wholesome goodness and is perfect to use in smoothies.

1 handful of kale
1 handful of baby spinach
1 avocado
Juice from 1 lime
¾–1-inch piece of fresh ginger, peeled
1 banana
1 apple
⁴⁄₅ cup (200 ml) orange juice
Water, to desired consistency

Process all the ingredients in a blender. Pour into four glasses.

TIP! You can vary flavors by using coconut water or apple juice instead of orange juice.

FOODPOWER by ANNA OTTOSSON

- SERVES 4 -

Run Forrest, run. The latest trend among runners is to load up on nitrates. By drinking green smoothies, you'll be able to run faster, longer, and harder because of the nitrates in the spinach.

2½ oz (70 g) baby spinach (1 bag)
1 avocado
Juice of one lime
¾–1-inch piece of fresh ginger, peeled
1 banana
1 handful of frozen mango
Splash of orange juice
Water, to desired consistency

Blend everything to a smooth consistency of a light-green color.

VITAMIN & DETOX WATER

You don't have to get by everyday with just plain water—this is deluxe water. Just add in other ingredients to make it taste fantastic and boost your health. Let it steep overnight or prep it in the morning, and bring it with you wherever the day takes you.

My everyday hero during flu season

GINGER WATER

- SERVES 2 -

I don´t step outside my door during flu season without warm ginger water. Drink it whenever you feel a cold coming on, and you just might be able to keep it away altogether. That's how powerful ginger is; it's a real jolt for your immune system!

4-inch piece of fresh ginger, peeled
2 ⅕ cups (500 ml) boiling water
½ lemon
1 tsp honey (optional)

Slice the ginger, place it in a bottle, and pour hot water over the ginger. Let it steep for 10 minutes. Squeeze in the lemon and add the honey, if desired. Refill the bottle with hot water throughout the day.

TIP! If you prefer a stronger ginger taste, grate the ginger instead of slicing it.

HOLY WATER

- SERVES 2, MAKES 2 BOTTLES -

Blueberry water full of antioxidants from the forest.

2 handfuls of blueberries
2½–3½ cups (600–800 ml) water

Split the berries between the two bottles and add the water. Let the bottles sit overnight in the refrigerator.

TIP! If you're impatient, like me, just grab a handful of frozen berries and put them in a glass of water. The blueberries will flavor the water immediately and vitalize it with powerful antioxidants.

DETOX WATER

- SERVES 2, MAKES 2 BOTTLES -

2 handfuls of fresh strawberries
1 lemon
½ bunch of mint leaves
2½–3½ cups (600–800 ml) water

Chop the strawberries into pieces to release more flavor. Slice the lemon, and rinse the mint leaves. Split the ingredients between the two bottles. Fill them up with fresh water, and let steep.

TIP! Always carry a bottle with you in your bag—for the car, the office, etc. As you hydrate throughout the day, you'll help your body flush out what it no longer needs.

ORANGE DETOX

- SERVES 2 -

1 orange
A handful of frozen blueberries
4 fresh stalks of mint
2½–3½ cups (600–800 ml) water

Slice the orange and put the pieces in a smoothie jar. Scatter with blueberries and mint. Fill the jar up with water, and let steep.

TIP! Freeze sliced fruit and berries and add frozen fruit to the water so it stays cold for longer on a hot day.

HERBS—Not Just a Garnish

- SERVES 2, MAKES 2 BOTTLES -

Herbalism is central to the philosophy of anthroposophy, and I've had the pleasure to work at an anthroposophy hospital in Sweden. The hospital has its own organic herb garden, a paradise of healing herbs, such as borage, basil, dill, coriander, savory, mint, marjoram, parsley, rosemary, salvia, and thyme, to name a few. You can make herb water with any herb you like—just pick your favorite.

2 sprigs of fresh thyme
2½–3½ cups (600–800 ml) water

Rinse the herbs and place one sprig in each bottle. Add water, and let steep overnight in the refrigerator.

TIP! Make an herb slush. Gather your favorite herbs and mix them in some water with an immersion blender. Top up with additional water and transfer the herb slush to a bottle.

MINT WATER

- SERVES 2, MAKES 2 BOTTLES -

Hello, gorgeous! – your skin will be pampered!

6 sprigs of fresh mint
10 thin slices of cucumber
1 lime, sliced
2½–3½ cups (600–800 ml) water

Rinse the mint and split between the two bottles. Squeeze in the cucumber and lime slices, and fill with fresh water. Let steep overnight in the refrigerator.

RAINBOW WATER

- SERVES 2 -

Enjoy all of Mother Earth's natural colors—drink the rainbow!

1 orange
1 lime
½ pomegranate
4 sprigs of mint
1 handful of fresh blueberries
2½–3½ cups (600–800 ml) water

Slice the orange and the lime, and pick out the pomegranate seeds carefully, to avoid getting red stains all over the kitchen. Split with the rest of the ingredients between two tall jars or bottles and fill them with water. Let it steep, and enjoy the colors of the rainbow that are so good for you!

OH, IT'S HOT

- SERVES 2, MAKES 2 BOTTLES -

It is said that chili boosts fat metabolism. What is for sure is that this water will definitely increase your body heat; it's hot!

4 cinnamon sticks
2 red chilies
2½–3½ cups (600–800 ml) water

Split the cinnamon sticks and the chilies between two bottles, and fill them with water. Let steep in the refrigerator overnight.

POWER JUICE SHOTS

Friends with bite. They're perfect to have on hand when flu season is in full swing. Knock one back in the morning or whenever you feel the need for a powerful, healthy kick.

DOUBLE SHOT: Bye-Bye, Colds

- SERVES 2 -

8 black peppercorns
1 lemon
¾–1-inch piece of fresh ginger, peeled
¾–1-inch piece of turmeric root, peeled
½ orange

Put all ingredients through the juicer. Pour the juice into a glass and knock it back. For extra heat, top the shots with a few twists of the pepper grinder.

TIP! Ginger has superstar status in my kitchen because it's phenomenal at strengthening the immune system.

GINGER SHOT

- SERVES 2 -

1 apple
¾–1-inch piece of fresh ginger, peeled

Put these two "heroes" through the juicer.

ANAHATA SHOT

- SERVES 2 -

If I could bring only one juice shot to a desert island, this would be the one.

¾-1-inch piece of turmeric root, peeled
1 lemon
1 pear

Put the ingredients through the juicer. Pour it into shot glasses and sip. This lovely drink can also be made in larger batches to be drunk like juice.

TIP! Place your organic lemons in a water bath before juicing them. You can then save and freeze the peel to use for later when you feel like making broth.

TIP! Turmeric has an incredibly intense color. Be careful where you set down fresh turmeric root on a working surface as it stains tables and cutting boards easily. If you've already stained something, quickly cover the area with dish liquid, let it soak, then wash or scrub it off.

FENNEL SHOT

- SERVES 2 -

There's something special about fennel. The hint of licorice, along with the apple and ginger, makes this a shot you'll want to drink again and again.

2 apples, cored
1 chunk of fennel
¾-1-inch piece of fresh ginger, peeled

Put it all through the juicer!

IMMUNE BOOSTING SHOT

- SERVES 2 -

This is the tequila of the juice shot world. The orange, ruby red grapefruit, and ginger combo is a real "kill or cure" remedy. I've chosen to use oranges here because they are rich in vitamin C. Vitamin C isn't just a vitamin; it is also a very powerful antioxidant that strengthens our immune system.

1 orange
¾–1-inch piece of fresh ginger, peeled
½ ruby red grapefruit

Put all ingredients through the juicer. Serve the drink in small shot glasses, and accompany with a side of grapefruit segments to suck on, as you would after downing a tequila shot.

HEALTHY FIREBALL

- SERVES 2 -

Feel like a fire-breathing dragon! In Asia, dragons symbolize happiness and good fortune, and the Water Dragon is considered the most powerful of them all. The Year of the Water Dragon comes around once every seventy years, a time that sees more weddings celebrated and more children born. My youngest child is a Water Dragon.

¾–1-inch piece of fresh ginger, peeled
¾–1-inch piece of turmeric root
2 oranges
A pinch of cayenne pepper
Ground cinnamon

Peel the ginger, turmeric, and oranges. Process them through the juicer. Season as desired with cayenne pepper and cinnamon. Pour into shot glasses and then down the hatch!

BABY SHOT FOR NEWBIES

- SERVES 2 -

This could be a good starting point if you've never taken a juice shot before. This recipe is one of the milder ones in this book; you could even test it on the kids.

1 orange
¾–1-inch piece of fresh ginger, peeled
A handful of fresh pineapple cut into ¾-inch chunks

Peel the orange and the ginger, and cut off the hard, crocodile-like peel from the pineapple. Put it all through the juicer.

TIP! It'll be especially yummy to finish off your baby shot with a slice of pineapple.

EXTRA IMMUNITY BOOST! You can always add more ginger or turmeric to the shot for an extra boost.

HEALTH TONICS

These elixirs contain a wealth of antioxidants that strengthen your immune system. Health tonics apply the inherited traditional knowledge and wisdom of healing ingredients from the earth and different cultures in their recipes.

CHAGA-BAM-BOOM!

- SERVES 4 -

Madame Moustache Goes Chaga. A creamy health tonic made with the world's healthiest mushroom, chaga. This drink is the pinnacle of a green smoothie and antioxidant-rich chaga tea.

2½ oz (70 g) baby spinach (1 bag)
1 avocado
Juice of 1 lime
¾–1-inch piece of ginger, peeled
1 banana
1 handful diced mango
A splash of orange juice
⅘ cup (200 ml) chaga tea (see p. 91)

Place all the raw ingredients, plus the tea, in the blender. Blend!

CHIA FRESCA MADE WITH YOUR FAVORITE JUICE

- SERVES 2 -

What do you want to manifest in your life; what seeds do you wish to plant in your life today? Use your favorite juice in this book and make a simple Chia Fresca.

2½ cups (600 ml) of your favorite juice
4 tbsp chia seeds
Juice of 1 lime (optional)

Mix the juice and chia seeds in a pitcher, and add lime juice if you're using it. Leave the pitcher to cool in the refrigerator for at least 30 minutes. Stir with a spoon before serving.

TIP! You can make so much more than chia pudding with chia seeds—why not try a healthy chia drink? Chia seeds are naturally gluten-free and contain omega-3s, protein, and calcium, and they are also super rich in fiber, which is great for the gut.

ROSE WATER COCONUT KEFIR

- SERVES 4 -

Coconut water mixed with kefir is a light, refreshing health tonic brimming with wholesome lactic acid bacteria. It's perfect for balancing and strengthening the gut. Eighty percent of the body's immune response is in our gut. This tonic requires a bit of prep work because the kefir grains need to be "activated" before they can start producing all those good-for-you bacteria cultures that will make a happy gut. But I promise that it's well worth your time and patience!

1 quart (1 liter) unsweetened coconut water

4 tbsp kefir grains, activated (follow the instructions on the package if you buy nonactivated grains; they will take 5–7 days to become active)

2 tbsp rose water

1 cinnamon stick, or any flavoring ingredient (optional)

1 sterilized glass jar

1 kitchen towel

1 rubber band

Heat the coconut water to 98.6°F (37°C), or use it at room temperature. Pour the water into a large, sterilized glass jar, and add the activated kefir grains and rose water. You can also add a cinnamon stick or any other preferred flavoring ingredient. Cover the jar tightly with a kitchen towel and secure it with a rubber band. Don't cover the jar with a lid, because fermentation increases the pressure inside the jar. Leave the jar at room temperature for no longer than 24–48 hours. Strain or fish out the kefir grains. Store them according to the instructions on the packaging. Your kefir tonic is now ready to drink. Store in the refrigerator.

FLAVOR SUGGESTIONS:

You can leave out the rose water and flavor your kefir with the following (choose one per quart (liter) of kefir water):

2/5 cup (100 ml) pomegranate juice

1/5 cup (50 ml) lemon juice

SOME INFO ABOUT KEFIR GRAINS Kefir grains aren't actually grains, but really a mixture of yeast and bacteria. If properly looked after, they can be reused several times.

TIP! Metal utensils can be detrimental to the kefir, so it's best to use a wooden spoon when stirring the tonic.

TURMERIC TONIC

- SERVES 2 -

This wholesome health tonic is liquid gold! Turmeric's ancestry in the Indian Ayurvedic healing tradition goes back more than a thousand years. It's incredibly potent.

1½-inch piece of fresh turmeric root, peeled
2 oranges
2 carrots

Process everything in the juicer.

DOUBLE THE EFFECT Vary the strength of the tonic to suit your taste. If you want a stronger drink, use two pieces of turmeric. Black pepper and turmeric enhance each other's effect, so to double the potency, grind some fresh black pepper into the Turmeric Tonic. We're stronger together!

50 SHADES OF GREEN TONIC

- SERVES 2 -

This is a chlorophyll bomb.

1 handful of spinach
1 handful of kale
1 small piece of fennel
2 celery stalks
10 leaves of parsley
2 green apples, cored
1 tsp wheatgrass powder
1 tsp spirulina powder

Put everything except the wheatgrass and spirulina powder through the juicer, then whisk in the wheatgrass and spirulina. Chug it and feel the power of green!

MAGIC MUSHROOMS

- SERVES 4 -

This health tonic is inspired by Chinese medicine and ancient Asian culture.

2½ oz (70 g) baby spinach (1 bag)
1 avocado
Juice of 1 lime
¾–1-inch piece of fresh ginger, peeled
1 banana
1 apple, cored
⅘ cup (200 ml) orange juice
1 one-serving bag of reishi or lion's mane
Water

Blend all the ingredients together in a blender. Add water to achieve desired consistency.

TIP! You can add reishi or lion's mane to all the recipes in this book—both warm and cold drinks. It is a nutritional supplement that can be taken by anyone over eighteen years of age. It's available in health food stores.

East Asia's Secret Superfoods

Lion's mane and reishi are East Asia's secret superfood gems, magical mushrooms that strengthen the immune response. In these recipes, Asia meets Madame Mustache's green smoothies!

Reishi is a red mushroom that is rumored to be an excellent anti-stress remedy. It strengthens the immune system.

Lion's mane is a white mushroom that is sometimes called bearded hedgehog mushroom because it looks like it has a white beard. Lion's mane originates in traditional Chinese medicine. It is rich in protein and is said to enhance memory function.

SUPER SMOOTHIES &
TWO-LAYER SUPER SMOOTHIES

Rainbow goodness.
Eating and drinking all the vibrant colors of the rainbow is a great way to
combine all that is healthy and delicious into a single glass.

SUNSET SMOOTHIE

- SERVES 2 -

Colors as brilliant as a sunset over the sea's horizon. Perfect as a refreshing drink or a super delicious treat at the beach.

YELLOW LAYER

4½ oz (125 g) frozen mango
2/5 cup (100 ml) orange juice
Juice from 1 lime

PINK LAYER

4½ oz (125 g) frozen raspberries
1 frozen banana, chopped
2/5–3/5 cup (100-150 ml) almond milk
1 tbsp chia seeds
Mint leaves

Blend the two layers separately. Start by blending the yellow layer. Rinse out the blender, then blend the pink layer. Spoon the yellow and pink blends in layers in pretty glass jars or glasses.

THE SKY'S THE LIMIT

- SERVES 2 -

Blue antioxidants at their best. We call this "raw food ice cream" in our house, and the kids totally love to eat this healthy dish for breakfast. It can also be sipped as a drink or eaten as a smoothie bowl—in the latter case I sprinkle it with coconut flakes, almond butter, and fresh blueberries. Yummy!

9 oz (250 g) frozen blueberries
2 bananas
3/5–4/5 cup (150-200 ml) almond milk
Ground cinnamon, to taste
Ground cardamom, to taste

Place frozen blueberries, bananas, and almond milk in the blender. Flavor with cinnamon and cardamom. Blend to a smooth, blue cream and enjoy immediately.

MADAME MOUSTACHE'S HEALTHY INDULGENCE

- SERVES 2 -

GREEN LAYER
1 frozen banana, sliced
1 handful of kale
1 handful of pineapple
2/5 cup (100 ml) almond milk

PINK LAYER
4½ oz (125 g) frozen raspberries
2/5 cup (100 ml) almond milk
1 handful of strawberries
1 handful of pineapple, chopped

Blend the two layers separately. Start by blending the green layer and fill the glass half full with the green smoothie. Wash out the blender, blend the pink layer, and fill the glass to form two layers. You can do two or more layers, if you wish.

RAW CHOCOLATE NANA SMOOTHIE

- SERVES 2 -

So good you'll only hear slurping!

CHOCOLATE LAYER
3 frozen bananas, chopped
1 tbsp raw cocoa powder
Grated coconut, for topping
Raw chocolate cream (see p. 68 [optional])

RASPBERRY LAYER
4½ oz (125 g) frozen raspberries
1/5 tsp pure vanilla powder
½ tbsp chia seeds
2 tbsp orange juice

Begin with the chocolate layer: blend all the chocolate layer ingredients in the blender and then spoon the layer into glasses. Wash out the blender, blend the raspberry layer, and add into the glass.

TIP! I've eaten bananas all my life, but I had never eaten them frozen. The difference is amazing! Try it; you'll swoon!

CHOCOLATE SMOOTHIE WITH RASPBERRY TOPPING

- SERVES 2 -

Marry chocolate and raspberries, and you'll get a smoothie that will create fireworks!

CHOCOLATE LAYER

2 tbsp raw cocoa powder

5 dates, pitted

4/5 cup (200 ml) almond milk

Sea salt

1 banana

RASPBERRY LAYER

4½ oz (125 g) frozen raspberries

1/5 tsp pure vanilla powder

½ tbsp chia seeds

2 tbsp orange juice

Blend the chocolate and raspberry layers separately. Fill the glasses half full with the chocolate layer, and top them off with the raspberry layer.

TIP! In this smoothie, the chia seeds should go directly into the blender without having to be soaked first, that way all its super wholesome nutrients are released.

ACAI-RAIN FOREST LOVE

- SERVES 2 -

Acai, those incredibly iron-rich berries, grow in the Amazon. They're the perfect boost for a smoothie.

4/5 cup (200 ml) frozen mixed berries
(raspberries and blueberries)

2/5 cup (100 ml) acai berries

2/5 cup (100 ml) coconut milk

1 banana

Blend all ingredients in the blender. It's ready to sip!

CHOCOLATE HEAVEN

- SERVES 2 -

I am a chocolate lover, especially high-quality chocolate that's rich in super healthy nutrients. This is a little slice of heaven—feel free to indulge without guilt!

SMOOTHIE
3 frozen bananas
1 tbsp raw cocoa powder
$2/5$ cup (100 ml) almond milk

RAW CHOCOLATE CUSTARD
$2/5$ cup (100 ml) almonds
$4/5$–$1\frac{1}{5}$ cups (200–300 ml) water
½ avocado
8 dates, pitted
2–4 tbsp raw cocoa powder
A pinch of pure vanilla powder
Grated coconut, for garnish

First layer: smoothie. Blend frozen bananas, cocoa powder, and almond milk. Fill glasses halfway with the smoothie.

Second layer: raw chocolate custard: Blend almonds and water with an immersion blender. Add avocado, dates, cocoa powder, and vanilla powder, and mix. Add the custard to the glasses, and garnish this deliciousness with grated coconut. Turn off your phone to get rid of any distractions, and totally enjoy!

TIP! Here's a simple way to clean your blender: fill it halfway with lukewarm water and a drop of dishwashing liquid. Blend. Pour out the water and rinse carefully. Done.

CHOCOLATE MEETS AVATAR

- SERVES 2 -

Chocolate ♥ green. So good! This one will take your breath away!

CHOCOLATE LAYER

2–3 tbsp raw cocoa powder

5 dates, pitted

⅘ cup (200 ml) almond milk

Sea salt

1 banana

½ avocado

GREEN LAYER

4½ oz (125 g) frozen mango

1 handful of pineapple

1 handful of spinach leaves

⅘ cup (200 ml) orange juice

Start with the chocolate layer. Blend all the ingredients and pour into glasses. Wash the blender, and blend the green layer. Add it on top of the first layer.

SUNSHINE FROM SMOOTHIE PRINCESS

- SERVES 2 -

My daughter's absolute favorite smoothie!

4½ oz (125 g) frozen mango

⅖ cup (100 ml) orange juice

Juice from 1 lime

Blend all the ingredients. Enjoy drinking these rays of sunshine, and shine like a thousand suns!

JUICES, LEMONADES & HEALTHY SLUSHIES

A party chapter filled to bursting with vibrant nutrient-rich juices,
delicious lemonades, and refreshing slushies, with virgin alcohol-free options
perfect to serve at a garden party under blue skies.

VIRGIN MARGARITAS
- SERVES 2 -

I only drink alcohol during a few rare occasions over the year. I prefer getting my high from real ingredients and from meeting new people. In this book, you'll find a large selection of alcohol-free drinks. And whatever I choose to sip, I prefer to drink out of beautiful glasses.

3 pomegranates, seeds only
1 orange
2 lemons
10 ice cubes
Fine-grained salt

Put the pomegranate seeds, orange, and lemons through the juicer. Pour the juice into the blender with the ice cubes, and blend. If you want a drink with a bit of bite, moisten the rim of two cocktail glasses or small, pretty, richly colored Moroccan glasses, and dip the rims in some salt. Pour the drinks and raise a toast!

GIRL POWER

One of my favorites!

2 handfuls of red cabbage, julienned
2 apples, cored
2 lemons
¾–1-inch piece of fresh ginger, peeled

Put all ingredients through the juicer. Done! Pour into two chilled glasses and offer this nutrient-blast-in-a-drink to your BFF.

HEALING CITRUS

- SERVES 2 -

Ruby red grapefruit is so healthy that I eat it as is, in salads, or as I do here—juiced. Blood oranges, those sweeties, have a short growing season, but it's like tasting a little bit of heaven. This juice provides such a kick of vitamin C that it'll take you to the moon and back.

1 ruby red grapefruit
2 blood oranges
¾–1-inch piece of fresh ginger, peeled

Put all the ingredients in the juicer. Three, two, one, blast off!

BEET JUICE—
Run, Forrest, Run!
- SERVES 2 -

Lemon and green apple balance out the earthier flavor of beets in this great-tasting juice. It brings a spring to your step, and compels you to press on toward the finish line.

3 beets
1 handful of kale
1 handful of spinach leaves
1 small chunk of hothouse (English) cucumber
1 stalk celery
1 lemon, peeled
1 green apple, cored
¾–1-inch piece of fresh ginger, peeled

Remove the green tops from the beets (if still attached), and rinse the beets free of all grit. Cut them into pieces to make them easier to put through the juicer. Juice all the ingredients, starting with the beets first. Pour into beautiful wineglasses, and sip!

This is rocket fuel in a bottle, and it's perfect in runners' circles, but it gives us mere mortals a shot of wonderful stamina, too. I am a long-distance runner from way back, born with a pair of running shoes on my feet. It wasn't worth lacing up those sneakers unless there were several miles to cover, and my idea of Sunday fun usually consisted of a three-hour run on the asphalt! This is how it all began: my keen interest in nutrition and, above all, sports nutrition. How should we eat for optimal results?

GREEN LEMONADE My Dharma

- SERVES 2 -

I love lemonade, but what you find in grocery stores contains far too much sugar to be enjoyable. Here is a refreshing healthy drink that's is perfect for mingling.

1 lemon
3 apples, cored
2 stalks of celery
½ hothouse (English) cucumber
1 handful of romaine lettuce
Juice from 1 lime
Fresh mint leaves

Peel the lemon. Put all ingredients, except mint leaves, through the juicer. Pour into glasses and garnish with mint leaves.

GINGERADE

- SERVES 2 -

Another favorite. I love ginger but think ginger beer is too sweet. If you find the amount of ginger here to be too much, just use a bit less.

¾–1½-inch piece of fresh ginger, peeled
1 lemon
2 green apples

Peel the ginger and the lemon. Cut the apples into wedges. Put it all through the juicer.

GREEN JUICE
—It's Never Too Late
- SERVES 2 -

2 green apples, cored
2 stalks celery
5 whole kale leaves
1 lemon
½ hothouse (English) cucumber

Put everything through the juicer. Done!

ONE-MINUTE SLUSHIE
- SERVES 2 -

Slushies are refreshing favorites that are super simple to make at home. Prep one without any added sugar.

4½ oz (125 g) frozen mango
⅘-1⅕ cup (200-300 ml) orange juice

Blend. Enjoy this on a hot day!

KOMBUCHA, CHAGA TEA
& HEALING DRINKS

Zen Buddhists drink matcha tea to focus during tea meditation ceremonies. Matcha tea was brewed for Asian emperors, while the Mayas of South America enjoyed their own chocolate drink. Healthy drinks go way back in time, and when updated with new fresh ingredients, they can help us reach new heights within ourselves. They center us and make us put our inner strength to use in the quest for becoming radiant from within.

RAW KOMBUCHA

If you take the time to make your own kombucha, you may as well make a large batch, and then flavor it in different ways. I nickname my kombucha's scoby mama "Beyoncé," because it is amazing and a glowing goddess. If I ever take her to a Fermentation Festival, she will probably bring home all the awards.

BASIC RECIPE
FIRST BREWING

3½ quarts (3½ liters) water
8 bags organic green tea
⅘ cup (200 ml) organic sugar
1 kombucha culture (scoby)
1 sterilized glass jar
1 kitchen towel
1 rubber band
Set aside ⅘ cup (200 ml) of the kombucha culture (scoby)

Bring the water to boil in a large saucepan. Drop in the teabags and let them steep for about 15 minutes. Remove the teabags.
Stir in the sugar and mix well. Let the water cool down to room temperature.
Pour the water into a glass jar, and add the kombucha culture (scoby).
Tightly wrap a kitchen towel over the opening of the jar, and fasten with a rubber band so nothing unwelcome can get into the jar.
Place the jar in a warm and dark place in the kitchen—under the sink or above the refrigerator, for example. Leave the jar undisturbed for 7–10 days. Brewing time will depend on the temperature where the jar is kept. It can take as little as 7 days, but also up to 14 days.
While it's brewing, sample the liquid with a drinking straw to gauge when it's ready.
The kombucha is now ready to be consumed. However, I prefer to flavor the kombucha and brew a second time.

FACTS The scoby is used for brewing over and over again. Small "babies" are created in the necks of the bottles in which you make your brews, and that's perfectly normal. They are part of the healthy bacteria that are rumored to strengthen the immune system and balance your gut. When the brew is ready, remove the scoby to another jar and add ¾–⅞ cup (170-200 ml) of the kombucha liquid so you have it available for your next batch. (It's the same idea as when baking with sourdough—you save a small piece of the sourdough starter for the next batch, and the next, and so on.)
If the kombucha tastes too sour, you can add more sugar (this is food for the bacteria, and about half of it is used up during fermentation).

CAREFUL—KEEP THOSE MITTS CLEAN!
Make sure your hands are freshly washed and clean before you handle the scoby.

MANGO KOMBUCHA
- SERVES 4 -

For this recipe, you'll need a fermented batch of kombucha, which you will now ferment again to add flavor. This is a milder variation with mango flavor.

FLAVORING THE SECOND FERMENTATION
1 quart (1 liter) basic kombucha (see basic recipe, p. 86)

4/5 cup (200 ml) mango purée, made from fresh or frozen mango

Mix the mango purée with the brewed kombucha. Cover it with a lid and let ferment for 1–3 days, depending on how strong a flavor you want. Pour into bottles but leave a space at the top as the kombucha will continue to ferment in the bottle. Store the mango kombucha in the refrigerator. If kept well chilled, the drink will be good for up to a month.

TIP 1 Freeze mango purée in ice cube trays to have on hand for the second fermentation once the basic kombucha is ready.

TIP 2 You can add in ginger for an extra health boost; it's super tasty, too.

APPLE & GINGER KOMBUCHA
- SERVES 4 -

2 apples, cored

¾–1¼-inch piece of fresh ginger, peeled

1 quart (1 liter) basic kombucha (see basic recipe, p. 86)

Put the apples and ginger through the juicer. Mix the apple-ginger juice with the kombucha and stir. Cover it with a lid and let it ferment for 1–3 days, depending on how strong a flavor you want. Pour the kombucha into bottles but leave some space at the top as the kombucha will continue to ferment in the bottles. Store the Apple & Ginger Kombucha in the refrigerator. If properly chilled, the kombucha will keep for up to a month.

Three quick things about kombucha

HONEY: Do not use honey; white granulated sugar is best. A lot of the sugar disappears over the brewing process as it is used to feed the kombucha bacteria during fermentation.

MOLD: If you see white, blue, or green mold, get rid of the batch!

GREEN TEA: do not use tea flavored with bergamot (Earl Grey) or fruity tea as this can weaken the kombucha culture.

CHAGA TEA

A tea made from the magical healthy mushroom that tastes of vanilla and the woods. This recipe shows you how simple it is to brew your own chaga tea.

RAW CHAGA TEA FROM MUSHROOMS
1 piece of fresh chaga mushroom, approx.
1½ x 1½ inches (4 x 4 cm)
1 quart (1 liter) of water

Place the mushroom in a saucepan and add the water. Bring it to a boil. Let it simmer for at least 1 hour. The tea can be drunk warm or cold.

The first batch will be black like coffee. You can reuse the mushroom several times (about 5–6 times), but you need to cook it longer every time you reuse it. You can keep using the mushroom while it still gives off some color.

OVERNIGHT CHAGA When the chaga has been cooked once, you can put the piece in a thermos, add boiling water, and let it steep overnight. It will be ready when you wake up. Stash your thermos in your bag to carry with you throughout the day. Living a healthy lifestyle is easy!

TIP! If you harvest chaga mushrooms yourself, cook them immediately or dry them in small chunks in the oven at low temperature. Store the dried chunks or the powder in a glass jar.

CHAGA BOOST You can add chaga tea to your smoothie to give it an extra boost, even though it will add a taste a little woody or like vanilla. I like to drink chaga mostly as a tea or as an alternative to water.

ALMOND MILK

I love homemade almond milk because it's terrifically tasty; plus, it's so easy to make, taking only about 2 minutes. Why schlep almond milk home from the store, when it's mostly water with traces of almonds? I use this homemade almond milk as a base for my other drink recipes. Warmed up almond milk is a perfect way to unwind in your comfy chair at the end of the day, as you watch the rain pour outside your window. It wraps around your stomach like a cotton blanket.

2 handfuls of almonds (preferably roasted)
1 quart (1 liter) water
A pinch of sea salt
4 dates, pitted
A pinch pure vanilla powder

Blend it all together. Voilà! It's ready to drink. It will keep for a few days if stored in the refrigerator.

TIP! I have a soft spot for roasted almonds, but you can use raw almonds, too. Whenever my daughter and I roast almonds, we usually make a large batch. That way we have them readily available to be used as toppings for granola, or when a craving for almond milk strikes.

GOLDEN MILK

- SERVES 1 -

"Turmeric latte" is one of the many other names for golden milk. This superstar drink is a treasure, made from homemade almond milk and the oh-so-trendy ingredient in health circles, turmeric, which has long been part of the Indian Ayurvedic medicinal tradition.

1-2 tsp organic ground turmeric, or a 4-inch (10 cm) piece of crushed fresh turmeric
1 cup (250 ml) almond milk
A pinch of cardamom and cinnamon

Whisk the turmeric into some of the almond milk until it forms a paste. Add the remaining almond milk and the spices.
Heat up your golden milk, and drink it from a beautiful cup.

FACTS: Fresh turmeric looks like fresh ginger root, except that it's more yellow-orange in color. Turmeric is loaded with antioxidants and is a powerful anti-inflammatory ingredient. Curcumin, the active chemical in turmeric, has been shown to kill cancer cells in laboratory settings.

MATCHA TEA LATTE

- SERVES 1 -

Green matcha tea from Japan is well known for its abundant antioxidants.

1½ tsp matcha tea powder
1 tsp warm water
1 cup (250 ml) milk of your choice
1 tsp honey (optional)

With a small whisk, mix the matcha tea powder and the warm water directly in a cup until it is well blended. Heat the milk in a saucepan and beat until frothy. Pour the milk foam over the matcha in the cup and stir. Feel free to sprinkle some matcha powder on top of the tea.

TIP! Use a latte whisk to froth the milk. If you have the luxury of owning a coffee maker with milk frother, even better.

BABYCCINO

- SERVES 1 -

Cappuccino without the coffee

⁴⁄₅ cup (200 ml) almond milk
Ground cinnamon
Ground cardamom

Make milk foam as you would for a latte. Pour it into a gorgeous cup and sprinkle cinnamon and cardamom over the surface.

EXTRA LAVISH TOPPING: Maybe some raw chocolate shavings, or why not a pinch of raspberry powder?

GINGER & TURMERIC TEA

- SERVES 2 -

¾–1-inch piece of fresh turmeric
¾–1-inch piece of fresh ginger
1 lemon
2⅕ cups (500 ml) water
1 tsp honey
Freshly ground black pepper (optional)

Peel and slice the fresh turmeric and ginger, juice the lemon, and place it all in a large saucepan. Add the water. Let everything steep a little, and then bring to a boil. Add the honey. Add the black pepper if you wish to strengthen the effect of the turmeric.

LOVE
IS THE
NEW
BLACK

RAW MAYAN CHOCOLATE DRINK

- SERVES 2 -

*Chocolate should be dark as the night, organic, and, of course, fair trade.
This chocolate drink is as far from the sugary powdered chocolate
drinks of your childhood as you can get.*

2⅕ cups (500 ml) almond milk
2 dates, pitted
½ stick cinnamon, or ½–1 tsp ground cinnamon
½ vanilla bean
3½ oz (100 g) dark chocolate

Blend the almond milk and dates together. Pour into a saucepan, add the cinnamon stick or ground cinnamon. Split the vanilla bean lengthwise; scrape out the vanilla seeds and add them to the saucepan along with the bean. Heat everything up gently. Remove the cinnamon stick and vanilla bean from the hot liquid. Grate the chocolate and mix it into the saucepan, stirring thoroughly until all the chocolate has melted. Remove from the heat and serve in beautiful cups. If you use store-bought almond milk, you'll need to double the amount of dates to achieve the right balance of sweetness and chocolate. You can add some honey if you wish.

EVERYDAY LUXURY Serve strawberries with the chocolate—they're lovely for dipping.

TIP 1 Place a pat of your favorite nut butter (almond or peanut butter) into the chocolate drink to elevate it. One teaspoon of nut butter per cup is usually enough.

TIP 2 If you want a Johnny Depp-level of spicy—as in the movie *Chocolat*—add a pinch of chili powder, or use chili chocolate instead of regular dark chocolate.

EXTRA PROTEIN BOOST Do you want chocolate so thick that the spoon almost stands upright on its own in the cup? If so, whisk an egg into the warm chocolate, and serve immediately!

BROTHS

Nutritious broths are replacing lattes on the streets of New York City.
Broth is so much more than just a base for soup; it's really a concentrate of nutrients that
has been left to simmer slowly until it is reduced into a high-octane healthy drink.

CHICKEN BONE BROTH

- SERVES 6 TO 8 -

1 chicken carcass

Olive oil, for the pan

2 carrots, coarsely chopped

1 yellow onion, coarsely chopped

1 whole head of garlic (slice it across the middle through all cloves, leaving the peel on)

2 stalks of celery, coarsely chopped

1 sliced lemon

Parsley

$\frac{1}{5}$ tsp turmeric, ground

3 quarts (3 liters) water

Freshly ground black pepper

Salt

Sear the chicken carcass in a sauté pan coated with some olive oil. While you do this, mix the vegetables, lemon, parsley, and turmeric with more olive oil and roast them in an oven-proof dish at 435°F (224°C). Then, place everything in a large stockpot and cover with the water. Bring to a boil and let simmer—do not boil—for 4–6 hours.

Strain the broth, and pour the liquid back into the stock-pot. To make an intense broth, reduce the liquid by half by boiling it uncovered at a high heat. Season with salt and pepper. Pour the broth into jars once it has cooled down, and store it in the refrigerator or freezer.

FOUR QUICK THINGS ABOUT BROTH

1 For a lighter broth, do not sear the carcass and do not roast the vegetables.

2 Why not make a double batch of broth while you're at it? It takes the same amount of time, but you will have twice the amount of goodness.

3 There are broth fanatics who cook their broth for up to 30 hours to draw out every last drop of collagen, but 7 to 12 hours is more than enough. You can let the broth cook for a while, take a break, and then cook it again. It's the total cooking time that counts.

4 While the broth is chilling, a layer of fat will develop. You can keep it or scoop it off.

BEEF BONE BROTH FROM THE BRONX

- SERVES 6 TO 8 -

2¼ lb (1 kg) beef bones (marrow bones, thin ribs, oxtail bones)
1 carrot, coarsely chopped
1 yellow onion, coarsely chopped
1 parsnip, coarsely chopped
½ root celery (celeriac), coarsely chopped
1 leek, coarsely chopped (white part only)
2-3 quarts (2-3 liters) water
1 tbsp tomato purée
A few black and a few white peppercorns
2 tsp fresh thyme, finely chopped
2 tsp soy sauce
2 bay leaves

Roast the bones separately from the vegetables in a 435°F (224°C) oven for 40 minutes.
Put the carrot, onion, parsnip, root celery, and leek in a large stockpot and add the water to just cover the contents. Season with tomato purée, black and white peppercorns, thyme, soy, and bay leaves. Simmer, uncovered, over low heat for about 10–12 hours. Do not boil the broth. Strain the broth.
Reduce the liquid by half by cooking it uncovered. Season with salt and pepper. You now have a fantastic broth! Cool and store in jars.

VEGAN BROTH

- SERVES 6 TO 8 -

*Drinking a warm broth is like
receiving a big hug.*

1 yellow onion, coarsely chopped

1 leek, coarsely sliced

1 fennel bulb, coarsely chopped

2 celery stalks, coarsely chopped

1 parsnip, coarsely chopped

2 large carrots, coarsely chopped

1 whole head garlic (slice it across the middle
through all cloves, leaving the peel on)

Olive oil, to drizzle

3 quarts (3 liters) water

1 bay leaf

2–3 sun-dried tomatoes

Salt

White pepper

A bunch fresh herbs, whichever you prefer
(optional)

Spread all the vegetables and garlic on a baking sheet
and drizzle with some olive oil. Broil for 15 minutes
in the oven at 480°F (248°C). Place everything in a
large stockpot and add the water to cover the vegetables. Bring to a boil and let it simmer for 1½ hours.
Add the bay leaf and sun-dried tomatoes. Season with
salt and white pepper, and add the fresh herbs (if you
prefer).
Strain and cool the broth. Pour it into jars and store in
the refrigerator or freezer.

IMMUNITY BOOSTING BROTH

- SERVES 6-8 -

Imagine that you're home sick in bed, buried under the covers, and someone you love leaves this warming and healing broth at your doorstep or by your bedside. It's like a caress on your cheek. Isn't that just pure love?

2 quarts (2 liters) vegan broth (p. 107) (or one of the meat broths)

4-inch (10 cm) piece of fresh ginger

$\frac{1}{3}$–$\frac{3}{4}$-inch piece of fresh turmeric + 1 to 2 tsps dried turmeric

1 whole head garlic (slice it across the middle through all cloves, peel left on)

Chili powder, to taste

1 sliced lemon

Prepare the vegan or meat broth. Add the rest of the ingredients to the broth, and let it all simmer for 1½ hours. Strain, cool, and pour into jars.

TIP! Umami—the fifth taste after sweet, sour, bitter, and salty—is essential if you want to make a tasty vegetarian broth. Add any of these umami goodies to raise your broth to new heights: mushrooms, sun-dried tomatoes, nori, or kombu (algae).

MADAME MOUSTACHE'S GREEN BONE BROTH

- SERVES 2 -

Enjoy a warm, green bone broth!

1 clove garlic, peeled

Chili powder, to taste

½ yellow onion, chopped

A small piece of leek

Oil, for frying

1 small bunch broccoli

A handful of kale

1 celery stalk

A handful of spinach

A handful of Brussels sprouts

$\frac{4}{5}$–$1\frac{1}{5}$ cups (200-300 ml) bone broth or vegan broth

Salt

Freshly ground black pepper

Sauté garlic, chili, onion, and leek in the oil. Transfer to the blender and process with broccoli, kale, celery, spinach, and Brussels sprouts. Add the broth. If you have a very powerful blender, mix until the broth is warm, or pour it into a pot and bring it to a boil. Season with salt and pepper.

INDEX

THANK YOUs ♡

Jack & Agnes —You're the best thing that has ever happened to me ♡

Sara N. Bergman – No words can express my gratitude for the magic you created with styling this book. You're a truly talented artist; plus, you text like nobody else. But most of all, I love to walk arm-in-arm with you and dance with you on tables deep in the Swedish boonies.

A thousand thanks to the dream team: Cecilia Viklund, Kerstin Bergfors, and Anna Sodini at **Bonnier Fakta** and **Kai Ristilä** for a job incredibly well done. What drive, happiness, power, and, above all, heart. I will be forever grateful. **Helén Pe**—aside from being a superb photographer with a personality as strong as Pippi Longstocking's, I am also so grateful for your limitless enthusiasm for my ideas. It feels like you've walked a mile in my moccasins.

Kim at **Garage**—because you vroomed in smokin' hot on your bike and drank juice shots, and arm-wrestled with me with your love tattoo. Totally love it!

Josefin Madsen—for makeup and hair. Wow, thank you for being you and for bringing out my best-looking, glammest me. And for staying cool while I performed my French car parking technique.

Anna Herslow—for all marvelous dharma-anahata talks. What gift! What a privilege.

Sarah Jonsson—thank you for introducing me to my very first green smoothie. ♡

Hannah Lemholt—thank you, wonderful you, for lending me your picture for the collage. Thank you for showing us your amazing world through your eyes and your camera.

Marie Olsson Nylander—Sweden's very own Frida Kahlo; stylist, artist, and dear friend. A thousand thanks for letting us come by and use your wonderful garden.

Anders Martinsson, Magasin 36—thank you for letting us hang out, photograph, and enjoy your place, as well as all the settings you've created. You're a living legend in my eyes.

Pålsjö Boden, Barfota, Garage, the wonderful **Bergman family**—thank you for fantastic locations and for adding some lovely vibes to this book (my heart beats a bit faster), and many thanks to ceramic artist **Eva Bergvall, Form from Skrå**, for beautiful cups.

A deep thank you to Skyhorse—my dear US publisher who made it possible for this book to spread its wings. You have shared my message of Foodpower with people all over the world, the message of the amazing power and peace that food can provide.

My deep love and gratitude to Gurmukh Kaur Khalsa and Jeannette Melo Pelletier—who believed in me and gave me their fullest heartfelt support beyond what words can express. I bow to you. ♡

Last, but not least, *Mom and Dad,* because you gave me life! Love conquers all.

One last THANK YOU goes out to the people I have met, whether at a crossroads, a setback, or in success. Whether the encounters have been brief or long, they all have one thing in common—they have been important to me in my life and over my twenty years as a dietician. People who have supported and challenged me, believed in me, and who have guided and inspired me along the way. I close my eyes in amazement, with a loving heart and a big, big smile on my lips, and bow in full gratitude.

CONVERSION CHART

METRIC AND IMPERIAL CONVERSIONS
(THESE CONVERSIONS ARE ROUNDED FOR CONVENIENCE)

Ingredient	Cups/Tablespoons/Teaspoons	Ounces	Grams/Milliliters
Butter	1 cup = 16 tablespoons = 2 sticks	8 ounces	230 grams
Cheese, shredded	1 cup	4 ounces	110 grams
Cream cheese	1 tablespoon	0.5 ounce	14.5 grams
Cornstarch	1 tablespoon	0.3 ounce	8 grams
Flour, all-purpose	1 cup/1 tablespoon	4.5 ounces/0.3 ounce	125 grams/8 grams
Flour, whole wheat	1 cup	4 ounces	120 grams
Fruit, dried	1 cup	4 ounces	120 grams
Fruits or veggies, chopped	1 cup	5 to 7 ounces	145 to 200 grams
Fruits or veggies, puréed	1 cup	8.5 ounces	245 grams
Honey, maple syrup, or corn syrup	1 tablespoon	.75 ounce	20 grams
Liquids: cream, milk, water, or juice	1 cup	8 fluid ounces	240 milliliters
Oats	1 cup	5.5 ounces	150 grams
Salt	1 teaspoon	0.2 ounce	6 grams
Spices: cinnamon, cloves, ginger, or nutmeg (ground)	1 teaspoon	0.2 ounce	5 milliliters
Sugar, brown, firmly packed	1 cup	7 ounces	200 grams
Sugar, white	1 cup/1 tablespoon	7 ounces/0.5 ounce	200 grams/12.5 grams
Vanilla extract	1 teaspoon	0.2 ounce	4 grams